119

D0435851

SELF-CARE *for* CATS
(AND THEIR HUMANS)

~~~ A Feline's Guide to Living ~~~
the Pampered Life You Deserve

PROTECT YOUR ALONE TIME.
WITH CLAWS IF NECESSARY.

PATRICIA WASHBURN

ADAMS MEDIA

NEW YORK   LONDON   TORONTO   SYDNEY   NEW DELHI

Aadamsmedia

Adams Media
An Imprint of Simon & Schuster, Inc.
57 Littlefield Street
Avon, Massachusetts 02322

First Adams Media hardcover edition March 2019

For information about special discounts for bulk purchases, please contact Simon & Schuster Special Sales at 1-866-506-1949 or business@simonandschuster.com.

The Simon & Schuster Speakers Bureau can bring authors to your live event. For more information or to book an event contact the Simon & Schuster Speakers Bureau at 1-866-248-3049 or visit our website at www.simonspeakers.com.

Interior design by Victor Watch
Illustrations by Claudia Wolf

Manufactured in the United States of America

10 9 8 7 6 5 4 3 2 1

Library of Congress Cataloging-in-Publication Data has been applied for.

ISBN 978-1-72140-003-4
ISBN 978-1-72140-004-1 (ebook)

"Memory" songwriters: Andrew Lloyd Webber/Trevor Nunn/T.S. Eliot/Zdenek Hruby
"Memory" lyrics © Sony/ATV Music Publishing LLC, Songtrust Ave, The Bicycle Music Company

Dedication

For Felix and Flavia, with love and gratitude.

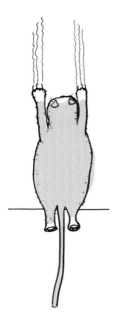

Introduction

Cats and humans have been getting along for ages. From Ancient Egypt to your very own living room, it's a relationship that's stood the test of time. But sometimes you need a little me(ow) time of your own.

By definition you are amazing, unique, and worthy of the best, whether it's deli turkey or the finest sunbeam warming your back.

You were born knowing this, of course. Everyone is. But sometimes life gets to you. Maybe your companion spends more time watching TV than anticipating your needs. Maybe you have somewhere to be, but all you want to do is nap. Maybe dinner is *four minutes late*.

That's why self-care is so important. You deserve to put yourself first and anticipate your own needs; you'll be happier, healthier, and better able to focus on the things that matter the most to you. So if you want to indulge, go for it! Want to savor the simple things in life instead? Do it; you decide what self-care works for you! Craving company? Find a friend who likes the same things you do. Looking forward to some alone time? There's no shame in hiding out in your favorite spot. Anything goes, as long as you're spending some time taking care of *you*. So let's talk *Self-Care for Cats (And Their Humans)*.

Stretch!
It feels great
and keeps you in shape.

Find a place
you can call your own.

Reaffirm that you are a creature like no other.

Take a minute to find some peace. It's within you, wherever you are.

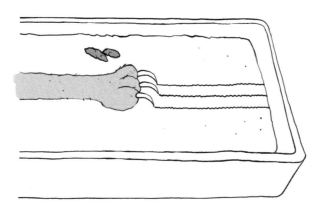

Live in the moment.
When inspiration strikes,
do what it tells you!

Protect your alone time.
With claws if necessary.

Practice meditation.

Play!
Try to see
the world with
childlike wonder.

Appreciate your body!

Get active.

Understand the
Law of Attraction.

Let go of anger.

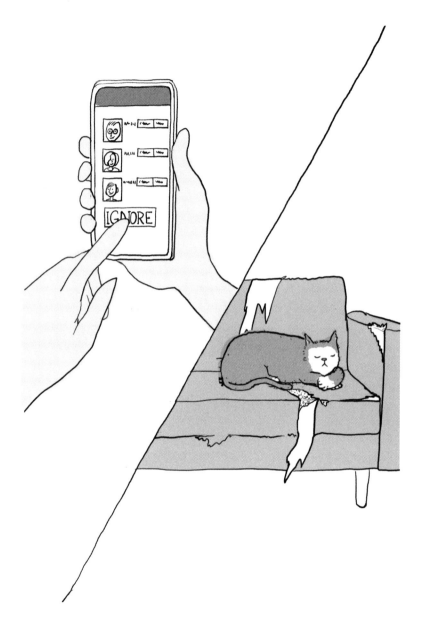

Appreciate the
simple things in life.

Do something
that scares you.
Go on, do it!

Feel your feelings!
Sometimes it's okay
to be upset.

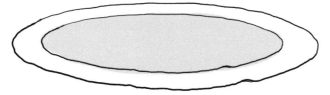

Don't take *no*
for an answer.

Respect yourself.
Walk away from those
who don't treat you well.

Enjoy a bath.

Make your bed.
Set a good tone
for the day.

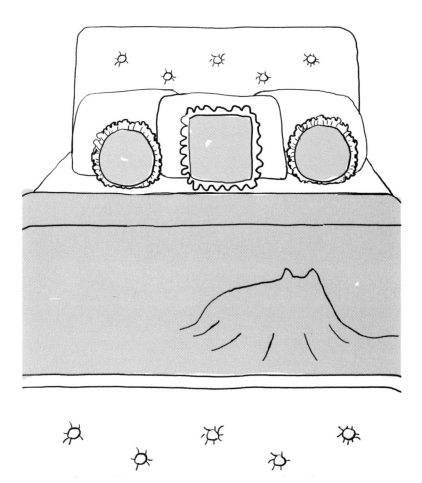

Embrace physical contact.
Nothing is more peaceful
than snuggling with
someone you love.

Don't dwell on your mistakes. You'll get it right next time!

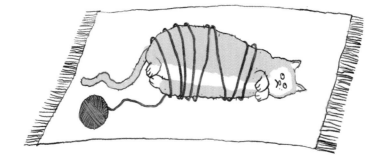

Cancel plans!
Sometimes staying home
is the best thing
you can do.

Write a letter to a friend. Knowing how much they'll enjoy a personal note will fill you with good feelings.

Create a calming
bedtime ritual.

Drink plenty of water!

Stay focused
on your goals.

Practice random
acts of kindness.

Take a mental
health day.

Spend time in nature.

Sing! Even if your voice isn't concert quality, singing stimulates your body and mind—and it's fun too.

Greet every day
with promise.

Spend time with your friends. Even hanging out at home can be fun.

Practice patience.
Good things come
to those who wait.

Share what you have
with others.

Manage your screen time.

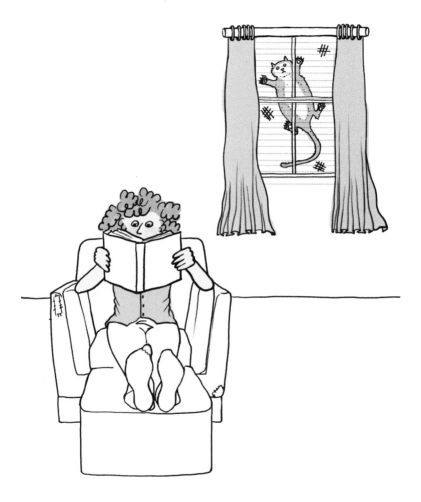

Aspire to great heights!

Engage with the present.

Take care of a plant.

Let someone brush your hair—it's relaxing!

purr

Increase your
fiber intake.

Find a mentor.

Apologize to someone.

Spend time with
a sick friend.

Express yourself through art. Never mind whether others understand it.

Vary your normal route and notice what's different. You may gain a useful new perspective!

Change your mind.
If your old favorite
things have lost their
charm, explore and
discover new ones!

Get away for a change of scene. You'll appreciate home all the more when you get back.

Challenge yourself.

Make new friends.

Go for a run.
Get those
endorphins flowing!

Don't be afraid to indulge. You deserve it.

Don't let a closed door
stand in your way.
If you want something,
figure out how to get it.

Declutter.

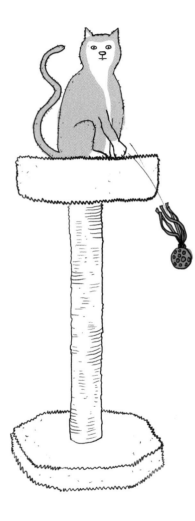

Watch the clouds go by.

Get plenty of sleep. You'll wake up feeling rejuvenated and ready to face the day!

Eat more superfoods.

Listen to your
favorite music.

Find your balance.

Celebrate with your
best friend.

Acknowledgments

Thank you to all the cats and cat people in my life, and to Cate and Katie at Adams Media for shepherding this little book!

About the Author

Patricia Washburn has been cat staff since before there was an Internet. She is not a crazy cat lady because the threshold for that title is two more cats than you already have. When not writing about cats, Patricia writes about cybersecurity, software, and large scientific building projects. As a single female writer of a certain age, she is practically required to have cats. She currently is supervised by two former shelter kittens.